CALL OF THE NORTHWOODS

CALL OF THE
NORTHWOODS

David C. Evers & Kate M. Taylor

WILLOW CREEK PRESS
Minocqua, Wisconsin

© 2008 David C. Evers and Kate M. Taylor
For Photographer copyrights, see page 93.
Map on page 16 © Kathy Verner Moulton, Illustrator, www.kavooom.com

The authors wish to give a special thank you to Rod and Marlene Planck,
who operate Rod Planck Photography in McMillan, Michigan, for their
thoughtful attention to the photographs in this book.

Published by Willow Creek Press
P.O. Box 147, Minocqua, Wisconsin 54548

For information about custom editions, special sales, premium and
corporate purchases, please contact Jeremy Petrie at 800-850-9453 or
jpetrie@willowcreekpress.com.

Editor/Design: Andrea Donner

Library of Congress Cataloging-in-Publication Data
Evers, David C., 1962-
  Call of the Northwoods / David C. Evers and Kate M. Taylor.
    p. cm.
  ISBN 978-1-59543-614-6 (hardcover : alk. paper)
  1. Forest animals--Northeastern States. 2. Forest ecology--Northeastern States. 3.
Forests and forestry--Northeastern States I. Taylor, Kate, 1961- II. Title.
  QL112.E84 2008
  591.730974--dc22
                              2008001302

Printed in Canada

For Nicole, Danielle, Taylor, and Thomas:
Love these woods
and the wild they shelter

–Dave and Kate

Life celebrates itself upon the land.

–Jeff Fair

CONTENTS

Foreword

by Jeff Fair

THE CALL OF THE Northwoods? Yes, but which one? Which wood notes, what northern soundtracks, best inform our images and reflect our romance of the Great Northwoods? In my case, the list ranges from the classic to what some might consider the obscure. The midnight falsetto of loons. The dissonant harmonies of wolves. That old hoot-owl down on Tidswell Point. The motor-like whine of a quadrillion mosquitoes lifting out of the willows in dinner formation. Wind whipping through the pines. The hollow winnowing of snipe. One white-throated sparrow chanting his *Old Sam Peabody Peabody Peabody* mantra. The bellow, come September, of a rutting bull moose, which sounds as though someone were prying open the corroded door hinges of a rusted-out 1967 Dodge Powerwagon. The deep-throated, urgent peals of the mink frog, *Rana septentrionalis*, "frog of the North," so rarely acknowledged by my bird-watcher friends. Only the conversations of trout are less discerned. I love them all.

Yet there is another suite of North-wooden sounds just as memorable and appropriate but which lie outside the purview of this volume—except that I shall invoke a few examples here, to wit: That lovely cadence, echoing from afar, of someone splitting spruce rounds with an axe for her evening fire. Rain—or black flies—ticking against the brim of a felt fedora. The voices of Hastings and Ricardi and their guitars—*In the midnight moonlight midnight*—mixed with the crackle and splendor of their bonfire, all softly muffled by the surrounding forest. The preprandial clatter and swearing—"Ouch! Hah-*damn* dat's hot!"—of my friend Armand Riendeau out by his fire pit on the Rapid River in Maine, as he prepared his infamous *poisson fumé avec sauce au brocoli* (yellow perch smoked above his campfire in the housing of a discarded water heater with a can of condensed soup for marinade). Like other old-time guides and cooks of the Great Northwoods, Armand is gone now. He was an endangered species when I knew him, rarer than the Kirtland's *wobbler* he told me once himself.

And… that faint drumming from out across the lake of a trip of canoes paddling in the still of night after spending the day windbound. My own intimate romance of the Northwoods was kindled four decades ago in my earlier, more formative years (all my years are formative years) by this very sound on a dark July night in New York's Adirondack State Park. Two other staffmen and I, and nine campers from a venerable canoe camp over in Vermont (wood-canvas canoes, traditional Cree paddling techniques, etc.) had established ourselves on the shore of Waltonian Island. Late in the evening the two senior staff took it upon themselves to paddle to the mainland on a venture about which I was sworn to secrecy (though I still remember the women's names), leaving me on watch. The night was

still and I let our fire burn down to a few incandescent coals.

Out on the water I heard something, barely audible at first; not a whisper but a heartbeat. The syncopated drumming grew closer, and I soon recognized it as the sound of the two paddlers returning, the shafts of their paddles bumping the gunnels of their canoes with every stroke in true Cree style. Ash to ash, wood to wood, wooden paddle to wooden canoe—the heartbeat on the water. In that moment I came to know that humankind once was and can still be a natural and organic part of these Northwoods, of the real world, wild and beatific.

Twenty years passed, and then one night in a secret and solitary campsite on the shore of Aziscohos Lake in western Maine, I awoke to that same heartbeat again, this time accompanied by the lively tune of a fiddler in one of the canoes. I sat in silence and listened, mesmerized, as the ash and fiddle corps' music carried across the water for miles. Years later, after telling this story, my brand new friend Bill Zinny would ask, "Was it Saint Anne's Reel?" When I replied Yes, he said, "That was me."

The moral I labor toward is that we

need not look past our own kind for some of what calls us back to the Northwoods. In fact, until enough of us remember that we are part and participant of the landscapes we love, until we remember how to approach them with respect and reverence, with joy and appreciation and music— there will be no true land ethic, no complete conservation. Participation involves knowledge and understanding, something available from experience, a grandfather, or a field guide such as this. But it also requires an intimate connection, a willingness and desire to romance the land and those who dwell there. That part, dear reader, is up to you.

One more thing. The authors of this little Northwoods primer needed also to limit their geographic purview, but the reader and I do not, and much to be found in the following pages is applicable far and wide across the northern forests of this continent. For example, here by the Matanuska River in south-central Alaska, on a distant edge of the boreal forest, I live among spruce and birch, cottonwood and aspen and alder, mountain ash and highbush cranberry, fool hen and hare and hoot owl, red-backed vole and moose and bear. Far away in miles, but not much different in content and spirit from Sigurd Olson's northwoods, nor Robert Frost's.

These woods, too, bring me joy. This afternoon, while the sunset lingered in hot pink and salmon and violet low in the southwestern sky, I watched the ravens wing their way, croaking and clanking, back to a secret roost in the high country. A buzz of boreal chickadees has reappeared at my suet. The ermine who lived with me last winter has moved back under my cabin; I found his signature on the snow today. Now, in the final twilight, that same old fool moon sleds low across Pioneer Peak, silhouetting the steepled spruce and breaking trail for Orion. And what I am privileged to listen to at this moment is the hush of the hoarfrost, the music of the stars—a profound and crystalline silence. One more song not to be found in the field guides, but valid to the human heart as a reminder of a peace, wild and primeval, available to us in the dark and lovely woods. Wherever we may find them.

Jeff Fair
Winter Solstice, 2007
Lazy Mountain, Alaska

The Northwoods

A PLACE FOR ALL SEASONS

THE NORTHWOODS IS a place of both spirit and landscape. Here stands a forest of needle and leaf, of shade and brightness, of rock and ridge, of still waters and rapids, of ever-changing seasons. Dark coniferous forests of pine, fir, spruce, and hemlock in the North gradually give way to the colorful woods of aspen, birch, maple, and oak. Under these canopies echo the living sounds of the seasons: the croaking of ravens and wood frogs turn spring into summer. Loons call from wilderness lakes, while songbirds share their concerts in the leafy shade beneath a summer sun. The wild notes of whole congresses of swans, geese, and cranes from overhead herald the colors of autumn, only to quiet into the solitary hoots and howls of owls and wolves as winter snows and darkness descend on the Northwoods. To immerse ourselves deeply in these woods and their wild voices is to find pause and peace in a quickening world.

The Northwoods is a place to invest in the seasons. The release of winter to spring is gradual in this country. The measure of those that dwell here is an ability to withstand cold temperatures and even snowfall late into spring.

It starts with the first bare patch of ground, the graying of melting ice and the small rustle of new activity on the forest floor. April and May can be temperamental months in the Northwoods, but these are also times of great change. Frogs emerge from their deep sleep in time to welcome warblers arriving from distant places. And so begins a time of defining space, finding mates, locating dens, and weaving nests.

Summer brings warmer temperature and biting insects. Black flies appear first, followed by mosquitoes, "no-see-ums," deerflies, and horseflies. These insects are a rich nutrient source at a time when these woods surge with new pups, cubs, and hatchlings.

By September, spring changes are now in full reverse. The sun's influence wanes and nighttime temperatures begin to drop. This coolness will eventually bring new colors of red, yellow and orange to the landscape. Insects are slowed by the cold and this year's wildlife progeny will now undertake their first migration in search of richer food sources. Bird migrations are measured in weeks and the readying of many resident animals for the long winter will occur over the next several months.

In November, leaves felled from sharp winds fill eddies and back water. Soon, the first snowflakes will make their way through barren branches to gather on needles. The snow pack will build now and through the next few months, the lakes will lay frozen.

Some animals will wait out this period below ground; those who stay will need to be well equipped for winter's test. The solstice promises many weeks of freezing temperatures and harsh conditions ahead. Only the shimmering greens, blues and reds of the aurora borealis will temper the harshness of winter. In time, the first bare patch of ground will arrive once again.

What Are the Northwoods?

The Northwoods comprise a vegetative transition zone between the eastern deciduous forest of the United States and the boreal forest of Canada. American beech, black cherry and silver maple become rare, while more southerly tree species such as hickories, boxelder, sassafras, yellow poplar, and white oak disappear altogether. Trees that are distinctive components of the more mature forests in the Northwoods are comprised of white and red pines, balsam fir, yellow birch, and sugar maple. In the younger or *successional* stands, jack pine, quaking aspen, bigtooth aspen, and white birch are common. Black spruce and balsam poplar are boreal forest species that extend their range south into the Northwoods. One

species, the red spruce, is only found in the mountains of the Northeast, while another species, the jack pine, is primarily confined to the Great Lakes (with a notable disjunct population in Maine).

Where Are The Northwoods?

Delineations of the Northwoods vary greatly. While that vagueness may be disconcerting to a mapmaker, the idea that the spirit of the Northwoods easily moves across borders and other mapping conventions is encouragingly wild. The Northwoods can be described as a transition zone from the massive boreal forest ecoregion of Canada and the great deciduous forests of the eastern U.S. Most maps will show the northern limits of the Northwoods in southern Ontario, Quebec and much of the Canadian Maritimes. Our treatise of the Northwoods here emphasizes the southern part of the Northwoods lying within the U.S. border. This includes northeastern Minnesota, the northern half of Wisconsin, and in Michigan, the Upper Peninsula and the northern half of the Lower Peninsula. In the Northeast, New York's Adirondack Mountains are the heart of this region's Northwoods continuing east through Vermont,

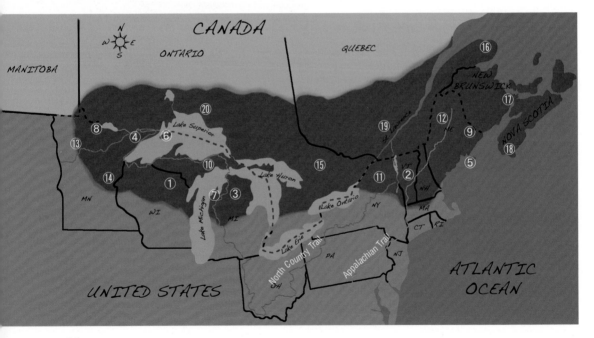

New Hampshire, much of Maine and small areas of Massachusetts.

This book focuses on the most prominent species found in the Northwoods. It is our opinion that the species within best embody the spirit and essence of this region.

Gallery of Northwoods Habitats
Pine Forest (P)
There are of three types of pinelands and all are associated with dry, sandy soils. Jack pine plains are most prominent in the Great Lakes and monotypic stands can cover large areas. This tree is closely tied to forest fires. Fire temperatures of 116° F soften resin surrounding the cone releasing heat-resistant seeds. Red pines are generally found mixed in with other conifers. Pure stands are rare and are mostly the result of plantings, common during the middle part of the past century. The outside bark of mature red pines is quite resistant to forest fires and larger red pines are some of the few trees left standing after a fire. Eastern white pines can reach heights of over 200 feet and are a signature species of the Northwoods. Although stands of old growth white pines are now rare, the

Sphagnum bog, Tahquamenon Falls State Park, Michigan

remaining stands are inspiring reminders of the Northwoods of old.

Sphagnum Bog (B)
The Northwoods is at the southern periphery of extensive sphagnum peatland bogs that extends north throughout much of Canada. While bog areas on the U.S. side are far less expansive, they are more than a novelty. Northwoods bogs reach over 500 square miles in Minnesota and over 4,000 acres in New York and Maine. This land-

scape feature attracts a unique set of flora and fauna. Sphagnum mosses are common, responding to the low availability of minerals and acidities. In some cases, sphagnum moss can cover an existing waterbody creating "quaking bogs." Black spruce and tamarack are the most regularly occurring tree in this habitat. Other distinctive woody vegetation in bogs includes shrub species such as Labrador tea, bog laurel, and leatherleaf.

Below: Spruce-fir forest; opposite: pine forest

Spruce-Fir Forest (SF)

This forest type characterizes the Northwoods. It has a boreal forest component more commonly associated with areas across the border in Canada. In the U.S., the spruce-fir forest is more rare than in Canada, however boreal wildlife communities are still present. In the Great Lakes, the white spruce is found in upland areas, while the black spruce dominates the wet acidic soils of bogs. In New York and New England a third species, the red spruce, is also present and is found in montane areas. Balsam fir is regularly associated with these spruces, especially the white and red species.

Northern Hardwood Forest (NH)

Forests dominated by sugar maple, yellow birch, eastern hemlock and balsam fir create a mix of deciduous and coniferous trees that encompass large areas of the Northwoods. These mixed forests are common in upland areas. When stands reach a mature state in 50 years or more, the closed forest canopy reduces the ability for vegetation to grow on the forest floor.

Lakes, Ponds and Wetlands (L)

Lakes are a prominent feature of the Northwoods. The action of retreating glaciers 10,000 years ago helped create the extent and distribution of most lakes in this region. Lakes and ponds are either spring fed (*seepage lakes*) or created by pooling surface waters (*drainage lakes*). Characteristic of many lakes in the Northwoods are deep, clear waters, otherwise known as *oligotrophic* systems. Such lakes typically have an abun-

dance of zooplankton that sustains a relatively robust fish and wildlife community. Lake edges are typically comprised of wetlands with sedges, cattails and bulrushes.

Rivers and Streams (R)

The Northwoods is the origin of many major rivers, including the Mississippi and smaller systems such as the Connecticut, Hudson, and Penobscot Rivers. In this region, rivers are fast-flowing and lack the wide floodplains

typical of more southern rivers. Waters flowing from cedar swamps and wetlands often have a brownish color, marked by natural tannins.

White Cedar Swamps (WC)
The northern white cedar forms continuous, sometimes pure stands in lowland and lakeshore areas of the Northwoods. This dis-tinctive forest community is well known for providing a protective canopy during the winter for white-tailed deer. Along parts of the Great Lakes shoreline, white cedar is mixed with fir, spruce and birch, creating attractive habitat for a wide range of breeding warbler species. In the Northwoods, small and relatively isolated stands of the Atlantic white cedar are present along the ocean shoreline of Maine.

Northern hardwood forest

Grasslands and Open Areas (G)
Vegetated natural openings and cleared forested areas are common across the Northwoods. Wet sedge meadows are associated with natural disturbances, such as those created by beaver activities and fires. Although grassy plains in dry areas can reflect naturally shallow soils that inhibit tree growth, most are the result of clear cutting followed by intensive fires that have burned the soil's organic matter. This action slows forest recovery, so much so that former stands of old growth white pine forests may remain barren over a century later. Pastures and old fields also represent long-term manipulation of the land. When left alone, forests eventually reclaim these openings.

Above: Century-old opening at the Kingston Plains, Alger County, Michigan

Left: Sharp-tailed Grouse, such as this courting male, gather in breeding groups called *leks*. This species requires large openings to support breeding populations.

21

Water and Rock

There are some areas of the Northwoods that are not defined by vegetation. They are instead known for their bare rock and water. The Great Lakes shoreline is one of these areas. Lake Superior is the largest freshwater lake in the world (by surface area) and has a commanding connection with the Northwoods in Michigan, Minnesota, Wisconsin and Canada. It includes long stretches of sand beaches, painted sandstone ledges, and rugged boulder-strewn shores. Lake Michigan to the southwest and Lake Huron to the southeast share many of these grand features, but lack the majestic quality that Lake Superior's deep, clear waters hold.

Rocky outcroppings are minor components in the Great Lakes region, but become prominent in New York and New England. There, the highest mountain peaks retain snow late into the summer; lichen and moss covered bedrock replace trees. Maine, New Hampshire, New York and Vermont all have mountain peaks over 4,000 feet high and support open alpine habitats. Further east is another special Northwoods feature—the Atlantic Ocean's Gulf of Maine. Much of this coastline is comprised of rocky shores and protected coves of sand and pebbles. Coniferous forests of spruce and fir border this unique part of the Northwoods.

Top: Grand Sable Dunes,
Pictured Rocks National Lakeshore, Michigan
Bottom: Cobblestone beach and Otter Cliffs on the
Atlantic coastline, Acadia National Park, Maine

Signature Species of the Northwoods

While the diversity of wildlife in the Northwoods is less than that found in tropical ecosystems, the sheer numbers of individuals is astounding. In some areas, the Northwoods forest floor can contain over 6,000 salamanders per acre. Recent estimates of continental bird populations indicate tens of millions of individual songbirds rely on the Northwoods. The black-throated blue warbler, for example has a breeding population of nearly two million individuals in this region alone.

Over 300 species of terrestrial mammals, regularly breeding birds, reptiles, and amphibians currently occupy the Northwoods in the U.S. Nearly one-third of the most notable species are covered in greater detail in this book. The general location, season of occupancy, habitat type, and population status are provided for selected signature Northwoods species (see *Codes for Species Accounts*).

Emerging fiddleheads and mosquitoes
are part of the signature sights and
sounds of the Northwoods.

Codes for Species Accounts

Location:
GL–Great Lakes
NY–New York
NE–New England

Occupancy:
PR–Permanent Resident
S–Summer
M–Migratory
W–Winter Visitor

Habitat Type:
P–Pine forest
B–Sphagnum bog
SF–Spruce-Fir forest
NH–Northern hardwood
forest

L–Lakes
R–Rivers and streams
WC–White cedar swamp
G–Grasslands and open
areas

Population Trends:
I–Increasing
D–Decreasing
S–Stable

Audio Sign:
🔊–Signature sound
can be heard on
enclosed CD

Spring
IN THE NORTHWOODS

One swallow does not make a Summer,
but one skein of geese cleaving the mark
of March thaw, is the Spring.

–Aldo Leopold

Large-flowered trillium, Michalsen Preserve (The Nature Conservancy)
Door County, Wisconsin

Black Bear (Ursus americana)

Location: GL, NY, NE; Occupancy: PR;
Habitat Type: SF, NH, WC; Population: S to I

Black bear feature prominently in the many national and state protected areas of the Northwoods. Bear-proof containers found throughout parks and campgrounds are a good indication of their presence. An interest in trash undermines a bear's true nature to methodically search for wild food. In the Northwoods, bears spend the winter in a semi-hibernation state where their bodies experience lowered metabolic rates. Hollowed logs, cliff ledges, and fallen trees all create protective areas for overwintering

Black Bear

bears. Two cubs are typically born in mid-winter and emerge in April with their mother. Males are independent and do not contribute to raising the young. The bear family has few predators and both cubs survive unless food is limited. Although black bear will opportunistically predate small to mid-sized mammals, they prefer insects and plant material, including berries. Black bear families remain together for two full seasons.

Expect to find black bears across a wide range of the Northwoods and in many habitats. Black bear populations have held steady in the northern United States. Populations of black bear coexist with people in rural areas.

Wilson's Snipe (Gallinago delicata) 🔊

Location: GL, NY, NE; Occupancy: S, M;
Habitat Type: B, L; Population: S

The courtship flight sounds of the Wilson's snipe are heard in open wetland areas throughout the Northwoods, especially from mid-April through the end of May. Air moving through specially designed outer tail feathers creates a "winnowing" sound. The male makes this sound while flying 100 to 200 feet above his territory to attract a mate. While perched, the male also makes a *tika tika tika* call. Once a female accepts him, the male ends his courtship flights. Four eggs are laid in a ground nest and are only incubated by the female. The chicks hatch nearly three weeks later and are *precocial*; they are fully feathered and can leave the nest immediately. Snipe have an unusual parenting strategy: upon hatch, the male and female split the brood and independently raise two chicks each. Snipe families feed on wetland invertebrates, such as insects, earthworms, and snails. By early September, snipe have started their migration to southern U.S. and Central American wintering areas.

Expect to find this shorebird during *crepuscular* hours (dawn and dusk) when they are most active. The winnowing courtship sounds can even be heard at night. At a distance, such sounds are similar to the bouncing calls of the boreal owl.

American Woodcock *(Scolopax minor)* 🔊
Location: GL, NY, NE; Occupancy: S, M;
Habitat Type: NH, L, G; Population: S to D

The return of the American woodcock to small openings in the Northwoods is a sign of winter transitioning to spring. Starting in March, the male signals his presence by a

Wilson's Snipe

American Woodcock

nasal peent given just after sunset. Initiation of the courtship flight is designed to attract a listening female. Once in flight, the male will quickly gain in altitude. The twittering sound from his wings ends at the peak of the 250- to 300-foot flight. The woodcock then begins a zig-zag flight to earth, silently landing next to the female. In May, four eggs are laid in a leafy depression on the ground. Incubation and all other parental duties are solely the responsibility of the female. Within three weeks, the precocial chicks hatch. For these hatchings, their small size at ground level invites high predatory pressure. In September, woodcock have begun the fall migration back to their southern U.S. wintering areas.

Expect to find woodcock throughout much of the Northwoods, although their well-camouflaged plumage make them difficult to find outside of springtime. Breeding habitat includes alder thickets and other shrubby areas with small openings. A plentiful supply of earthworms and beetle grubs are captured underground by probing with a prehensile bill tip. The woodcock nightly eats its weight (¼- to ½-pound) in earthworms or other invertebrates.

Spring Warbler Migration

The Northwoods holds 28 species of breeding wood warblers. This group of birds can be described as relatively small, colorful, and highly vocal. Their wide range of songs and calls can be challenging to beginning birders. Sorting through the seemingly similar and endlessly interruptive sounds can be accomplished through patience and persistence. Time will provide an ability to more readily identify these birds by ear.

All Northwoods warblers are migrants. Some overwinter in the tropics (see *Northwoods Spotlight – Where is Home?*), while others remain in the southern United States. Spring warbler migrations are famous for their numbers, diversity of species, and vivid colors. Nearly all of the spring migrant warblers breed in the Northwoods. Their return to these woods is staggered according to species, natural rhythms, weather, habitat, and geography. There are few more rewarding moments than the discovery of a group of migrating warblers flitting within an aspen stand. Flashes of bright oranges from blackburnian warblers mix with the deep yellows of magnolia warblers, contrasting with the fresh mint green of new aspen leaves.

Magnolia Warbler

Blackburnian Warbler

Chestnut-sided Warbler

Spring Return Chronology of Warblers

The following weekly periods correspond with an approximate return chronology of Northwoods warblers. Although migrants can be found across all habitat types, species are separated here by general habitat choice.

Time Period	Coniferous Forest	Mixed Woods	Deciduous Forest
April 8-15	pine warbler	–	–
April 16-23	yellow-rumped warbler	–	Louisiana waterthrush
April 24-30	palm warbler	–	–
May 1-7	Nashville warbler	northern parula; northern waterthrush; black-throated green warbler; prairie warbler	common yellowthroat; ovenbird; American redstart; black-and-white warbler
May 8-15	Kirtland's warbler; Cape May warbler; magnolia warbler	blackburnian warbler	yellow warbler; Canada warbler; chestnut-sided warbler; black-throated blue warbler; Tennessee warbler; golden-winged warbler
May 16-23	blackpoll warbler; bay-breasted warbler	Connecticut warbler	Wilson's warbler; mourning warbler

Frog Spring Chorus 🔊

Some of the earliest spring awakenings are by *amphibians*, cold-blooded animals that spend the winter hibernating under frozen water and mud. Even the slightest warmth and opening of water begin to stir frogs. There is a methodical procession of frog species that transition from their near frozen hibernacula to lively spring choruses (see *Northwoods Spotlight – Parade of Frog Calls*). The first frog sounds from vernal pools, ponds, and lakes in the Northwoods are the quacking calls of wood frogs. Often, these frogs are calling next to ice and snow. Soon, diminutive spring peepers make their mark, usually in massive numbers with familiar peeps that can drown out the calls of fellow frog species. Boreal chorus frogs, restricted to the Great Lakes region, are heard intermittently and are soon followed by the more widespread American toad. The trills of toads can be overwhelming when large numbers take over a marsh. The progression of frogs soon includes four look-a-like species, including a distinctive Northwoods species called the mink frog. This frog has a unique call that can sound like horse hooves clicking over cobblestone. The largest species, the North American bullfrog, and the two gray treefrog species bring up the rear of the procession.

Although unheralded, frogs are a critical component in the foodweb of aquatic ecosystems. A global decline of frogs, including many species in the Northwoods, is an alarming recent trend. A mix of stressors are likely responsible, including introduced fungal infections, contaminants, and climate changes.

From left: Wood Frog
Spring Peeper
Chorus Frog
American Toad
Northern Leopard Frog

From left: Pickerel Frog
Gray Treefrog
Green Frog
Mink Frog
Bullfrog

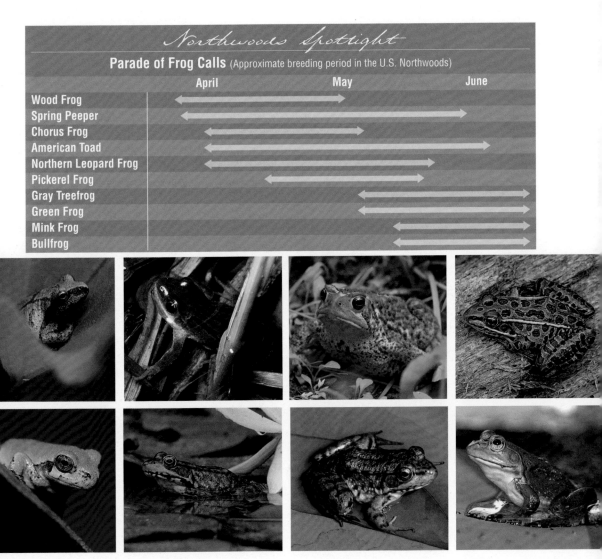

Northwoods Spotlight

Parade of Frog Calls (Approximate breeding period in the U.S. Northwoods)

	April	May	June
Wood Frog			
Spring Peeper			
Chorus Frog			
American Toad			
Northern Leopard Frog			
Pickerel Frog			
Gray Treefrog			
Green Frog			
Mink Frog			
Bullfrog			

Summer

IN THE NORTHWOODS

The creation of a thousand forests is in one acorn.

–Ralph Waldo Emerson

Island on a wilderness lake,
Boundary Waters Canoe Recreational Area, Minnesota

SUMMER IS A season rich in animal life, particularly vibrant in birdsong. This abundance in birdlife is best described in five general habitat categories including pine forests, open bogs, spruce-fir forests, northern hardwood forests, and lakes and ponds. Mammals covered in these pages are habitat generalists and therefore are not grouped in these categories.

Red Squirrel *(Tamiasciurus hudsonicus)* 🔊
Location: GL, NY, NE; Occupancy: PR;
Habitat Type: P, B, SF, NH, WC; Population: S

The red squirrel is strongly connected with pine, hemlock, and spruce cone crops. Although they will also eat berries, vegetation, and even small birds, their success in an area is primarily linked with cone crops. When cones are abundant, red squirrels respond by increasing their reproductive potential, often producing two litters versus the usual one. Telltale signs of red squirrel activity are mounds of cone scraps chewed into pieces in an effort to extract pine or spruce seeds. Red squirrels like to use habitual feeding posts and will establish food caches of cones. In the eastern Northwoods, red squirrels eat 45 to 50 cones a day. When red squirrel densities reach high levels, predation pressures on songbirds are more noticeable. In New York and New England, breeding populations of the Bicknell's thrush can be negatively impacted by red squirrel predation.

Expect to find red squirrels in areas of good cone production, although their chattering is easily heard throughout the Northwoods. They are abundant in campgrounds, often tamed enough to be fed by hand. Bird feeders filled with sunflower seeds will surely include a daily dining by red squirrels.

Red Squirrel

Gray Wolf *(Canis lupus)* 🔊
Location: GL, NE; Occupancy: PR;
Habitat Type: P, B, SF, NH, WC; Population: GL = I

The gray wolf is one of the more storied residents of the Northwoods. By the mid-

1900s, wolf populations were nearly exterminated across the United States from both fear and ignorance. Government bounties were in place for decades until this practice was finally abolished in 1965. Only one small population in northeastern Minnesota survived this period. In 1973, wolves were granted full protection under the U.S. Endangered Species Act. Since then, wolves have recovered to over 3,000 individuals across northern Minnesota, Wisconsin and Michigan's Upper Peninsula. Wolves in New York and New England are still rare and likely represent wandering individuals with Canadian origins. Reintroductions of wolves in the western United States, such as in Yellowstone National Park, have been successful. Such efforts in the northeastern United States are now being considered.

Gray wolf populations can recover quickly. This ability lies in being an apex predator with great reproductive potential. Wolves live in packs with a strict social hierarchy. The highest ranking, or *alpha* pair produce four to 10 pups that are cared for by the pack and weaned in seven weeks. Primary prey include ungulates, such as the white-tailed deer and moose. Research into predator-prey dynamics have found that the wolf tends to select young, weak, sick and old individuals, a strategy that enhances the overall fitness of prey populations.

Expect to find gray wolves by sound. Their deep howls are legendary and are

Northwoods Spotlight
Movement on the Forest Floor 🔊

Some small mammals, like eastern and least chipmunks, are readily heard and viewed while dashing across trails and visiting picnic tables. Many other small mammals are harder to find. Patience, silence and stillness can provide great rewards in these small sightings. In the Northwoods, the southern red-backed vole is a common rodent found in bogs

Eastern Chipmunk

and spruce-fir forests. The short-tailed shrew, deer mouse, meadow vole, and both species of jumping mouse are ubiquitous across the region. Both species of flying squirrels are surprisingly common but rarely seen. Some species are quite habitat-specific, such as the southern bog lemming in bog habitats and the rock vole in the mountains of New York and New England. Many small mammals are active year-round and require deep snows to guard against frigid temperatures and predators.

Gray wolf

Coyote

synonymous with the Northwoods. Wolf howls communicate the location and status of a wolf or wolf pack.

Coyote *(Canis latrans)* 🔊
Location: GL, NY, NE; Occupancy: PR; Habitat Type: P, B, SF, NH, WC, G; Population: S to I

The coyote is a relatively recent addition to the Northwoods mammal community. Coyotes are primarily a species of prairies and desert, but with the opening of the eastern forests, these canids spread into much of the Northwoods by the early 1900s. Concurrently, the gray wolf was being exterminated in this region. The removal of the gray wolf cleared the way for the coyote to fill their ecological niche as a primary predator.

Time has shown that the coyote is quite adaptable to changing habitats and new areas. In New England, coyotes have responded well to their new Northwoods home; they have increased in overall size and weigh an average of 50 percent more than their western counterparts. Some males may weigh over 60 pounds. Today it can be difficult to differentiate a New England coyote from a gray wolf. One identifier is the coyote's howl. Instead of the deep,

long howl of a gray wolf, the coyote has many high-pitched yips and yelps while howling. Calling occurs mostly at night, though they can be heard howling at any time. Coyotes use underground dens or other protected areas in April to birth young. An average of six pups are born, although a dozen or more pups may be produced during periods of dense prey populations. Pups are weaned after five to seven weeks. Coyote are opportunistic in food choices; small to mid-sized rodents and other mammals comprise the bulk of their diet in summer. In winter, deer can be important food sources. Family groups remain together into the winter.

Expect to find coyotes throughout much of the Northwoods, although the recovery of the gray wolf in the Great Lakes has tempered the size of coyote populations.

Pine Forest

Signature birds of pine forests in the summer are the spruce grouse, hermit thrush, Kirtland's warbler, and dark-eyed junco in jack pine plains; common nighthawk and red crossbill in red pine savannah areas; and pine warbler in white pine stands.

Spruce Grouse *(Falcipennis canadensis)* ◀))
Location: GL, NY, NE; Occupancy: PR;
Habitat Type: P, B, SF; Population: S

The spruce grouse or "fool hen" is an unusually tame bird. Courting males strut along hiking trails with red brows raised, buffy-tipped tails fanned and black upper breast feathers puffed forward. Often they fly up to a nearby tree to strut along a limb and then fly back to the ground. Such courtship antics are typical in the early morning. A thorough search may find a well-concealed female in a nearby spruce or pine.

Spruce grouse are famous for their strict winter diet of conifer needles, one of the few

Spruce Grouse

species able to survive on such food. Spring courting areas are often littered with droppings of partially digested pine needles. In summer, they switch their diet to insects. Only the female incubates the four to seven eggs for three weeks. Young can fly after one week but remain with the female for several weeks. If threatened, she will use a distraction display to protect the chicks from

potential predators. In the first year, young will move on average one to two miles away from their hatching sites. Once they find a nearby open territory, they will stay in that area throughout their lives. Most spruce grouse do not live past seven years of age.

Expect to find this grouse in three habitat types: jack pine plains, mountain ridges, and spruce-fir bogs. Courting arenas are usually sandy and free of vegetation.

Hermit Thrush *(Catharus guttatus)* ◀))
Location: GL, NY, NE; Occupancy: S, M;
Habitat Type: P, B, SF; Population: S

The spring return of the hermit thrush brings one of the most beautiful calls back to the Northwoods. This song can best be described as a twirling flutelike sound that fades to an end. Unlike other thrushes, the hermit thrush has a shorter migration from southern U.S. wintering areas. Such close proximity makes it one of the first migrant songbirds back to the Northwoods, usually by mid-April. Four eggs are laid in loosely knit cup-shaped nests placed low in the forest understory or on the ground. Upon hatch nearly two weeks later, both adults tend to the chicks, which fledge in another

---

Northwoods Spotlight
North vs. South

Birds are some of the most prominent wildlife in the Northwoods. Although birds that tend to have more northerly ranges are highlighted in this book, more southern ranging birds are just as abundant and often better known. Widespread southern species and their northern counterparts include the following.

Southern Species ⟶	Northern Counterpart
Virginia rail	yellow rail
Cooper's Hawk	northern goshawk
ruffed grouse	spruce grouse
hairy woodpecker	black-backed woodpecker
American crow	common raven
blue jay	gray jay
least flycatcher	yellow-bellied flycatcher
white-breasted nuthatch	red-breasted nuthatch
black-capped chickadee	boreal chickadee
yellow warbler	palm warbler
rose-breasted grosbeak	evening grosbeak
American goldfinch	pine siskin
swamp sparrow	Lincoln's sparrow

two weeks. Hermit thrushes eat invertebrates and sometimes salamanders in the summer. During winter and migration they feed on fruit.

Expect to find this thrush across many habitat types. They prefer dry forested areas such as pine or oak, but are also found in spruce bogs.

Dark-eyed Junco *(Junco hyemalis)*
Location: GL, NY, NE; Occupancy: S, M, W; Habitat Type: P, B, SF; Population: S

The dark-eyed junco is widespread across the Northwoods, commonly breeding in young pinelands, sphagnum bogs, and young spruce-fir forests. In June, females lay three to five eggs in a shallow depression on the ground. Incubation is undertaken solely by the female and lasts nearly two weeks. Young fledge over a week later. Like many sparrows, the junco feeds on insects for more protein in the summer, but switches to a seed diet for the rest of the year. Some individuals may remain throughout the year at the southern fringes of the Northwoods. In winter, flocks are formed of 30 or more individuals where a ranking system is established. The more dominant birds have greater

Hermit Thrush

Dark-eyed Junco

control over food and other resources, while subordinates perch at the edge of a feeding station waiting their turn to feed.

Expect to find the dark-eyed junco, or "snowbird," on the ground near birdfeeders during the winter.

Red Crossbill *(Loxia curvirostra)*
Location: GL, NY, NE; Occupancy: S, M, W;
Habitat Type: P, B, SF; Population: S

Red Crossbill

The red crossbill is a steady traveler, always searching for fresh new cone crops. The *jip-jip* notes heard while flying are often the first sign of their presence. Crossbills tend to travel in flocks spreading out across the upper reaches of a tree, working cones with their signature mandibles crossed at the tips. These specialty bills are used to remove the heavy outer cone covering. The seed tucked inside is then scooped out with their tongues. This behavior is reminiscent of parrots as they turn upside down to gain an optimal angle while feeding. Such an adaptation has served the crossbill well; it is widespread across the Northwoods.

Red crossbills have a habit of breeding where there is a bumper cone crop. Due to their nomadic lifestyle, flocks from New England are often mixed with others from the Great Lakes or with individuals from as far away as British Columbia. Cup-shaped nests are built high in the outer branches of conifers and lined with lichen, moss and feathers. Three to four eggs are laid and incubated for two weeks by the female. Young chicks will fledge two to three weeks later after being fed regurgitated seed pulp homogenized into a milky substance.

Expect to find crossbills in the winter, as they are most readily observed in this season. A drive down a snowy, gravel road in winter can find crossbills picking up grit to help digest cone seeds.

Sphagnum Bog

Signature birds of open bogs in the summer are the yellow rail, northern harrier, olive-sided flycatcher, palm warbler, and Lincoln's sparrow. Spruce-lined bog edges will include the yellow-bellied flycatcher, rusty black-

Northwoods Spotlight

Rarest of them all: Kirtland's Warbler

Kirtland's Warbler

The entire breeding range of the Kirtland's warbler is in the Northwoods of Michigan and Wisconsin. In winter, these birds are limited to the Bahama Islands. Their breeding biology is wholly tied to one habitat type: young jack pine stands that are four to 20 years of age. Jack pines, otherwise known as the "tree of fire," cannot release their cone seeds without the high temperatures created through fire. With human habitation, large areas of jack pines were cleared and wildfires were suppressed leaving little for these warblers. Further compounding such habitat loss was competition from a non-indigenous species, the brown-headed cowbird. This blackbird is native to open prairies and was able to expand eastward with the removal of forests. Cowbirds are *brood parasites*; they lay eggs among the eggs in other birds' nests. They then depend on the host species to incubate and raise their young. Cowbird young have rapid growth rates and out-compete young Kirtland's warblers.

The entire Kirtland's warbler population numbered 167 singing males in 1987. Twenty years later, the population of singing males has jumped tenfold to 1,697. This is a testament to carefully planned efforts by many individuals, organizations, and agencies.

bird, and white-throated sparrow. Sandy pine ridges are likely to harbor the common nighthawk, red crossbill, and pine warbler.

Northern Harrier *(Circus cyaneus)*
Location: GL, NY, NE; Occupancy: S, M;
Habitat Type: B, L, G; Population: S to D

The northern harrier is an open country raptor commonly seen gliding low over pastures, wet meadows, marshes, and bogs while hunting. This hawk has a facial disk similar to an owl. Such an appearance enables it to search for prey more by sound than sight. The harrier specializes in preying on voles but also captures other small mammals, birds, snakes, and frogs.

Male harriers make their spring return to the Northwoods in April. Females arrive after the males. Following a brief aerial courtship flight, the pair build a ground nest in dead grass cover, laying an average of five eggs. Up to nine eggs may be laid if prey are abundant. Eggs hatch after one month. Since the female begins incubation after the first egg is laid (as opposed to waiting until all eggs are laid), the first and last harrier chick may hatch over one week apart. Males can pair with more than one female and when eggs hatch, will provide

Northern Harrier

Common Nighthawk

food for the young of each nest. Male chicks fledge in four and one-half weeks while the heavier females leave at six weeks. Family groups remain together for up to one month after fledging. Harriers move south of the Northwoods for the winter.

Expect to find this raptor in most any open area particularly at times of high prey abundance. Harriers can spend up to 40 percent of daylight hours in flight.

Olive-sided Flycatcher

Common Nighthawk *(Chordeiles minor)* 🔊
Location: GL, NY, NE; Occupancy: S, M;
Habitat Type: P, B, G; Population: D

Common nighthawks are found in open pine savannahs, bogs with sandy ridges, and other open habitats. Nighthawks give a nasal *peent* call throughout the summer. During courtship displays, males emit a hollow booming sound using flight feathers while swooping toward the female. Two olive-white eggs are laid in a sandy depression and are primarily incubated by the female. Incubation lasts nearly three weeks and the downy hatchlings fledge three weeks later. Nighthawks are strictly insect eaters, preying on moths, flying ants, beetles, and mosquitoes. Individual nighthawks can eat hundreds of insects in one night. During late summer and in migration, nighthawks can be found in large flocks. Sometimes hundreds of individuals will gather in open areas to feed on outbreaks of flying insects. Nighthawks are long-distance migrants overwintering in South America.

Expect to find the common nighthawk most active at dusk. Having adapted to city life, they also build nests on rooftops.

Olive-sided Flycatcher *(Contopus cooperi)* 🔊
Location: GL, NY, NE; Occupancy: S, M;
Habitat Type: P, B, SF; Population: D

The olive-sided flycatcher's emphatic *quick, three-beers* is well known to visitors of open bogs in the Northwoods. These flycatchers are one of the last migrants to return in the

Boreal and Montane Breeding Bird Specialties for Birders

For dedicated birdwatchers, the Northwoods represents an opportunity to observe indigenous species at the southern fringe of their North American breeding range. Highlights for summertime birders include: spruce grouse, yellow rail, great gray and boreal owls (northeastern Minnesota), black-backed woodpecker, yellow-bellied flycatcher, gray jay, boreal chickadee, and the Connecticut warbler. These species are mostly found in spruce-fir forests associated with sphagnum bogs. In New York and New England, they also inhabit mountain slopes. In higher elevations, where spruce growth is stunted, Bicknell's thrush and blackpoll warblers are found. In New York, these birds are found above elevations of 3,600 feet, while in Maine both can be found at elevations as low as 2,600 feet. Higher yet, on the few mountaintops with open rocky terrain (such as Mt. Katahdin in Maine and Mt. Washington in New Hampshire), isolated populations of the American pipit breed. Tour leaders for birding groups and recently designated birding trails are helpful in identifying likely locations for viewing these prized species.

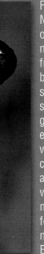

Black-backed woodpecker

spring, often not appearing until late May or even early June. Their lengthy migration route from wintering grounds in Panama and South America's Andes Mountains is the longest for North American flycatchers.

The olive-sided flycatcher times its arrival with the proliferation of flying insects, specializing in bees and wasps. For a songbird, the male defends a fairly large territory of 25 to 50 acres. An open cup nest made of twigs and lichen is built by the female, often 20 to 40 feet in a coniferous tree. While only the female incubates the three eggs for two weeks, both adults take part in feeding the young, which fledge in just over two weeks after hatching.

Over the past few decades, this flycatcher has dramatically declined throughout its range. Since flycatchers use disturbed forests, their decline is puzzling. Recent evidence, however, indicates a potential preference for forest opening created by fire instead of logging. They are a newly listed threatened species in Canada and are of high conservation concern in the United States. Efforts to understand this poorly studied species are now underway.

Expect to find this large flycatcher in

open bog habitats, jack pine plains, conifer clearcuts, and mountain ridges.

Spruce-Fir Forest

Signature birds of spruce-fir forest tracts in the summer are the spruce grouse, merlin, boreal owl, great gray owl, black-backed woodpecker, yellow-bellied flycatcher, common raven, gray jay, boreal chickadee, Cape May warbler (as well as over 10 other warbler species), white-throated sparrow, and white-winged crossbill. On mountaintops of New England and New York, residents include the Bicknell's thrush and blackpoll warbler.

Merlin *(Falco columbarius)* 🔊
Location: GL, NY, NE; Occupancy: S, M; Habitat Type: B, SF; Population: S to I

The merlin is one of the fastest raptors in the Northwoods sky. These birds are falcons and as such, they are well equipped for the speed needed to catch other birds on the wing. Prey commonly includes similar-sized birds such as the northern flicker and evening grosbeak. Merlins prefer to hunt along the edges of lakes, rivers, or open bogs, taking advantage of smaller birds crossing open areas. After returning in mid-

Merlin

spring from the southern U.S. and Central America, merlins choose abandoned crow, raven, or hawk nests in spruce trees. The female primarily incubates four to five eggs for a month. Upon hatching, young will need another four to five weeks to fledge. They remain with the adults for several more weeks for aerial training.

Expect to find these birds in boreal spruce areas that border open water. A high-pitched and repeated *kik-kik-kik-kik* call is a good indicator that a territorial merlin is present. Merlins are not common in the United States and in some areas, such as Michigan, they are a threatened species.

45

Gray Jay

Common Raven

Gray Jay *(Perisoreus canadensis)* 🔊
Location: GL, NY, NE; Occupancy: PR;
Habitat Type: P, B, SF; Population: S

The gray jay is one of the more conspicuous birds of the Northwoods. Like the red squirrel, these birds are easily tamed and aptly earn their nickname, "camp robber." Gray jays are far less vocal than their more southerly cousin, the blue jay. Gray jays have a unique behavior where they slowly glide from one tree perch to the next. Three to four eggs are laid early in March, while snow is still on the ground. The female incubates the eggs, with the male in attendance. He will feed her during this time, and their young. Young fledge in two weeks and are wholly black in color with a white eye stripe. A sharp ear may pick up contact calls between adults and their fledged young, often heard as a mix of shrill notes and cackles. Gray jays are permanent residents and spend their summers eating insects and fruit. In winter, they prefer carrion and can sometimes be found at suet feeders. Food is *cached*, or stored in conifers throughout the year.

Expect to find these birds in coniferous forests, among jack pine barrens, spruce-tamarack bogs, or in the montane spruce areas of New England. Gray jays are common in campgrounds and along hiking trails where they can be quite approachable.

Common Raven *(Corvus corax)* 🔊

Location: GL, NY, NE; Occupancy: PR; Habitat Type: P, B, SF, NH, WC; Population: I

The raven, like the common loon, is steeped in myth and legend. In some cultures, they are seen as messengers between this world and the spirit realm. Their physical attributes could attest to this role: ravens are found in the hottest of deserts, withstanding temperatures of 110° F or higher. They are also found in the coldest of regions, thriving even when the cold drops below -30° F. Ravens are often the only bird left in the sky during extreme weather. A raven's high intelligence is well worth noting. Bernd Heinrich found that ravens have an innate ability to problem solve. Perched birds in his study learned how to access food hung on a string by reeling it in with their feet and bills.

Ravens are early nesters, finding sites in trees and cliffs by March or April. Three weeks later, four to six eggs hatch. Both adults care for the chicks, which fledge by six weeks. Family groups remain together throughout the summer as both parents teach young to feed and evade predators. Ravens are opportunistic foragers, often found over carrion near roads or in open landfills. These corvids are year-round residents in the Northwoods.

Expect to find ravens most anywhere in the Northwoods. These birds are very vocal. Close monitoring of a raven pair or family will reveal their speech abilities, which encompass over 30 different types of vocalizations.

Boreal Chickadee *(Poecile hundsonica)* 🔊

Location: GL, NY, NE; Occupancy: PR; Habitat Type: P, B, SF; Population: S

The boreal chickadee, like its black-capped cousin, is one of the hardiest birds in the Northwoods. Weighing only seven to 12

Boreal Chickadee

grams (the weight of no more than two quarters), this chickadee is able to withstand temperatures dipping below 0° F by utilizing several survival strategies. For example, boreal chickadees will group together within a tree cavity to conserve heat. They also have tight feather tracts that protect their skin from cold, and fluffing feathers produces additional air pockets for further protection. Chickadee pairs use abandoned woodpecker holes or other tree cavities for laying five to eight white eggs. Chicks hatch after two weeks of incubation by the female and fledge in the same amount of time. Boreal chickadee families remain together until late fall. Although some chickadees disperse, most individuals are year-round residents.

Cape May Warbler

Expect to find the boreal chickadee in coniferous forests interspersed with aspen. Listen for the familiar *chick-a-dee* call, which is lower pitched and more nasal than the black-capped chickadee.

Cape May Warbler *(Dendroica tigrina)*
Location: GL, NY, NE; Occupancy: S, M;
Habitat Type: B, SF; Population: D

Cape May warblers are richly colored birds of yellow and green with chestnut-colored cheek patches. These warblers will choose a singing perch on the top of a spruce tree deep in a bog or boreal forest. Their song is a high and thin-pitched *seet seet seet seet*. Cape May warblers overwinter in the West Indies and begin their spring migration by making over-water flights to Florida in April, arriving at their breeding territories in mid-to-late May. Open cup nests, 30 to 60 feet high in spruce fir crowns, hold an average of six to seven creamy white eggs. Up to nine eggs are laid if food is abundant, such as during spruce budworms outbreaks. Few other warblers are known to lay such large clutches, which explains this species' ability to have widely fluctuating populations. Approximately one month after the last egg is laid, young Cape May warblers fledge from their nests. By late August, individuals have moved south of the Northwoods reaching their wintering island habitats in the fall, changing to a diet of nectar and fruit in coffee plantations and gardens.

Expect to find the Cape May warbler singing and catching insects from the top of spruce trees in areas with a strong boreal forest character. During years following spruce budworm outbreaks, this is a fairly common warbler.

White-throated Sparrow

White-throated Sparrow *(Zonotrichia albicollis)*
Location: GL, NY, NE; Occupancy: S, M; 🔊
Habitat Type: B, SF, NH; Population: D

For birders, the phrase *Old Sam Peabody Peabody Peabody* has been used to describe the melodic and distinctive song of the white-throated sparrow. This bird commonly sings throughout the day, amplified from an elevated perch. Such pronounced vocals can expose this small bird to predators, but it is the singing that will invite a potential mate and define a territory. Scientific findings indicate that males singing regularly and longer are most attractive to breeding females. White-throated sparrow

nests are constructed on the ground in habitats that range from clear-cut forests to boreal spruce bogs. This ability to adapt to various habitats makes the white-throated sparrow one of the more abundant species in the Northwoods. The female incubates four to six greenish-blue eggs for nearly two weeks. Both parents feed the chicks spiders, insects, and seeds. Young fledge in just over one week. Fall migration begins in September and peaks in early October.

Expect to find this sparrow across much of the Northwoods. White-throated sparrows are readily seen while singing or hopping along a path searching for insects and seeds. Try making a *pishing* sound near or within a breeding territory to attract the attention of males in the area. If interested, one will fly close making a sharp *chinking* call.

Northern Hardwood Forest

Signature birds of the northern hardwood forest in the summer include the broad-winged hawk, ruffed grouse, northern goshawk, great-horned owl, barred owl, whip-poor-will, yellow-bellied sapsucker, pileated woodpecker, great crested flycatcher, winter wren, wood thrush, veery, Swainson's thrush, blackburnian warbler (along with over 15 other warbler species), scarlet tanager, and indigo bunting.

Ruffed Grouse *(Bonasa umbellus)* 🔊
Location: GL, NY, NE; Occupancy: PR;
Habitat Type: NH; Population: S

Ruffed grouse are active throughout the year in the Northwoods. In spring, this normally quiet grouse makes its presence known. While perched on a fallen log, the male makes a low, hollow drumming sound by beating its wings against the air. Drumming starts slowly and accelerates in cadence until it reaches a rapid beat. This courtship action attracts female grouse, which are able to find and then evaluate the male's fitness. If the male is successful, he will mate with multiple females and have no further parental responsibilities. The female creates a nest depression in leaf litter, lines it with breast feathers, and lays an average of nine to 12 eggs. Hatching typically occurs 24 days later and the precocial chicks leave the nest upon hatch. Although young are able to fly in 10 to 12 days, they will remain with the female into fall. Ruffed grouse primarily forage on buds, leaves, flowers, seeds, and fruits. Insects are also eaten, especially by the chicks. Many predatory birds and mammals depend on the ruffed grouse for prey.

Expect to find ruffed grouse in mixed deciduous and coniferous forests with a strong preference for aspen stands. In spring, grouse perch in aspen trees eating buds. In summer, females are found along roadsides using distraction displays while hurriedly directing young to remain together. Fall is a time when grouse are most easily flushed and observed. In winter, when snows are deepest, ruffed grouse will spend the night burrowed in snow.

Northern Goshawk *(Accipiter gentilis)*
Location: GL, NY, NE; Occupancy: S, M, W;
Habitat Type: SF, NH; Population: S to D

Northern goshawks are large forest-dwelling raptors, difficult to find in their North-woods homes. These raptors have red eyes

Ruffed Grouse

Northern Goshawk

and an overarching brow giving them a look of apparent, and well-deserved, fierceness. Goshawks have significant talons for catching large prey. Snowshoe hares, red squirrel, and ruffed grouse are favored. Goshawk populations will fluctuate with the availability of these prey species.

In April, trees with large forks near their main trunk are preferred sites for nesting. Stick nests are built over 30 feet high in these trees, and in May, three to four blue-tinged eggs are laid. Female goshawks incubate the eggs for just over five weeks, while males bring food for them. During this period, goshawks are well known to be aggressive toward intruders, including people. A rapid, cackling *kye kye kye* call is given before striking at a threat. Although chicks will fledge between five and six weeks, it will take another month before they are truly independent.

Expect to find this raptor in areas with high densities of hare and grouse. Goshawks also prefer mature stands of mixed deciduous and coniferous forest that lack undergrowth. The brown streaked juvenile and subadults are more regularly seen than the adults.

Broad-winged Hawk

Broad-winged Hawk *(Buteo platypterus)* 🔊
Location: GL, NY, NE; Occupancy: S, M;
Habitat Type: NH; Population: S to I

The broad-winged hawk is the most commonly seen hawk in northern hardwood forests. These hawks make a high-pitched *tee-teee* whistle while lazily soaring over the forest canopy. Upon return from their wintering areas in Central and South America in late April, broad-winged hawk pairs choose a nest site in large deciduous trees. Once the stick nest has been constructed, two to three white-blue eggs are laid. Often a live aspen branch is brought to the nest and laid next to the eggs. Incubation is primarily by the female and lasts for over four weeks. Chicks fledge in five weeks and are fed by both adults. Prey items include a wide assortment of frogs, snakes, songbirds, and small mammals. During fall migration, the broad-winged hawk is famous for gathering in the hundreds and even thousands while riding thermals to their southern winter homes 4,500 miles away.

Expect to find this hawk breeding throughout the Northwoods. In summer, broad-winged hawks are commonly seen searching for prey while perched low on telephone wires along roadsides.

Great-horned Owl

Great-horned Owl *(Bubo virginianus)* 🔊
Location: GL, NY, NE; Occupancy: PR;
Habitat Type: P, SF, NH; Population: S

The great-horned owl is the nocturnal heavyweight of the Northwoods avifauna. Like the northern goshawk, these owls are well known for their fierceness, especially when protecting nests. The talons of great-horned owls can capture prey bigger than themselves, even as large as Canada geese, although moderately sized animals are preferred. This owl is one of the few species to regularly prey on skunk and will often take chicks from crow, raven, and raptor nests.

The calls of courting pairs can be heard as early as December, with characteristic hoots that can be identified by sex when pairs duet. The smaller males have a lower pitched *whoo who-whoo whoo whoo*, while the larger females respond with a higher pitched, *who-who who who*. Pairs use vacant stick nests near the tops of trees and lay two to three round white eggs. In four to five weeks, the eggs will hatch and the chicks fledge seven weeks later. Fledged young

Who's Calling? 🔊

There are several species of owls that call the Northwoods home, while others only visit in the winter months. The great-horned owl, barred owl, and northern saw-whet owl are the most common breeding species. The smallest of these three owls, the saw-whet, has a signature tooting call lasting for minutes at a time. The long-eared owl is a more rare breeding species, and gives a low single *hoooo* call.

During the winter, owl diversity changes. Although species such as the great-horned and barred owls remain, they are joined by a group of three northern forest owls. This trio is well-prized by birders and includes the great gray owl, northern hawk owl, and boreal owl. While the northern hawk owl is generally silent, the small boreal owl can be heard during the breeding season in April and May.

Northern Hawk Owl

Two open-country owls can also be found in the Northwoods. The rare and fairly silent short-eared owl is limited to open habitats rich with rodent prey in summer and winter. The tundra-nesting snowy owl is a regular inhabitant of the Northwoods in winter, particularly along the Great Lakes and Atlantic Ocean shorelines.

travel with the adults for several more months to learn hunting skills.

Expect to find the great-horned owl in virtually all Northwoods habitats. Crows will engage in *mobbing* these owls, a cooperative behavior where birds harass a potential predator to push it out of the area. Such events are a good way to find great-horned owls or other raptors. Beginning in June, listen for the young owls' unusual screeching call.

Barred Owl *(Strix varia)* 🔊

Location: GL, NY, NE; Occupancy: PR; Habitat Type: NH; Population: S

The barred owl is common in northern hardwood forests. This owl is easily identified with the characteristic *who cooks for you, who cooks for you-all* call. Pairs or family groups will also make noisy, barking and cackling calls. Barred owls use abandoned hawk and raven nests to hatch and raise young. Females incubate two to three white eggs for one month, during which time the male will provide food. After hatching, the chicks need seven weeks until they are ready to fledge. During this time, juvenile owls engage in *branching*, a behavior where young owls move outwardly along branches to gain confidence for flight while still receiving food from the adults. Barred owls prey on small mammals during crepuscular and nighttime hunts.

Expect to find barred owls in winter, particularly when food-stressed individuals begin foraging during the day. These owls are more difficult to spot in the spring and summer, though they are most vocal at this time.

Whip-poor-will *(Caprimulgus vociferus)* 🔊
Location: GL, NY, NE; Occupancy: S, M; Habitat Type: P, NH; Population: D

The whip-poor-will has a secretive nature and is rarely seen unless flushed from a roost. This bird's signature namesake call is their most recognizable feature. In June, a perched male begins to call at dusk, with his singing lasting late into the night. On these evenings, a repeated *whip-poor-will* can be heard hundreds of times. Egg laying is timed so young hatch one week prior to the full moon. By taking advantage of the ambient light available during this moon phase, whip-poor-wills have longer and more successful feeding bouts on moths, beetles, and other flying nocturnal insects. Two cream-colored eggs are laid on the leaf litter and

Barred Owl

Whip-poor-will

incubated by both adults for nearly three weeks. The downy hatchlings move in and out of the ground nest and by three weeks, will fledge. Whip-poor-wills overwinter in the southern U.S. and Central America.

Expect to find this species missing from some areas in the Northwoods. The reason for such declines is relatively unknown. In general, the whip-poor-will is a species of dry coniferous and deciduous forests, preferably with an open understory.

Pileated Woodpecker

Pileated Woodpecker *(Dryocopus pileatus)* 🔊
Location: GL, NY, NE; Occupancy: PR;
Habitat Type: SF, NH, WC; Population: I

The pileated woodpecker is a keystone species of the Northwoods. Their vacant nest cavities serve as important nest sites for other species, from common goldeneyes to northern saw-whet owls to flying squirrels. In spring, the pileated woodpecker is not just the largest woodpecker of the Northwoods, it is also one of the loudest. When calling to mark territorial boundaries, a loud and rapid series of ringing calls can be heard. A single *kuk* note is given when disturbed or interacting with another pileated woodpecker. Pileated woodpeckers are also well known for

their bill drumming. Repeated drumming on large dead tree limbs creates a commanding sound that easily resonates through the woods. Pairs remain together year-round, which is unusual for birds. In April and May, the pair will spend several weeks excavating a nest cavity. An average of four white eggs are laid and incubated by both adults for over two weeks. Chicks fledge two weeks later. When looking for food, such as beetle larvae or carpenter ants, pileated woodpeckers make characteristic rectangular carvings at the base of a tree.

Expect to find this woodpecker throughout the Northwoods. It is most visible (and audible) during the spring while bill drumming from a habitual tree and making its signature territorial call.

Winter Wren *(Troglodytes troglodytes)* 🔊
Location: GL, NY, NE; Occupancy: S, M;
Habitat Type: SF, NH, WC; Population: S

The diminutive, yet energetic winter wren packs a remarkable territorial song. The musical stream of notes and trills can last five to 10 seconds. For a tiny eight- to 12-gram bird, the tremendous song length and volume for its size makes it unique in the Northwoods. The male uses overturned trees or other tangled areas for camouflage during singing bouts. Once the pair returns from their southeastern U.S. winter retreat, five to six white eggs are laid in tree cavities or under stumps and uprooted trees. Like many wren species, the male will build several false or "dummy" nests that serve to confuse potential predators. Only the female incubates the eggs and feeds the young until they fledge after two and one-half weeks. Winter wrens eat spiders and insects.

Expect to find the winter wren as a common species throughout the Northwoods, although when not singing, this secretive and tiny songbird is hard to find.

Winter Wren

Northwoods Spotlight
Canopy Songsters 🔊

While walking through a mature stand of a northern hardwood forest, most bird sounds come from high in the forest canopy. Fewer bird species are found below this canopy level. Visual identification of songbirds at this height is difficult and as such, songs and calls are the best identifiers of these upper canopy inhabitants. One of these birds, the red-eyed vireo holds two records: it is the most common songbird in the Northwoods and it sings the most often. Individuals sing their *here I am, where are you* call up to 20,000 times per day. Other species of the forest canopy include the yellow-bellied sapsucker, great-crested flycatcher, blue-headed vireo, blackburnian warbler, and scarlet tanager.

Scarlet Tanager

Lakes, Ponds, and Rivers

The Northwoods is lake country. One state alone, Minnesota, is known as the "land of 10,000 lakes." Some of the signature waterbirds and wetland birds are Canada goose, trumpeter swan, common goldeneye, common merganser, hooded merganser, common loon, American bittern, great blue heron, osprey, bald eagle, Virginia rail, sora, sandhill crane, and belted kingfisher.

Trumpeter Swan (Cygnus buccinator)
Location: GL; Occupancy: S;
Habitat Type: L; Population: I

Trumpeter Swan

Trumpeter swans are native across the western half of North America. These birds are the world's largest waterfowl, weighing 20 to 30 pounds with a seven-foot wingspan. Sexes are similar. The trumpeter swan's history is marked by dramatic population declines due to indiscriminant shooting and loss of wetland habitat. In recent years, conservationists have made successful reintroduction efforts in former areas of the swan's breeding range.

Trumpeter swans are distinctive for their call that is best described as a powerful resonating "trumpet" that easily echos across a wetland or lake. These swans develop strong pair bonds that last throughout the year. This type of faithfulness is relatively unique for birds. Both adults work together to build large nest mounds of mud and sticks, some up to five feet in diameter, in open wetland areas adjacent to lakes. Abandoned muskrat houses are commonly used for a nest foundation. Four to six chicks hatch after a five-week incubation by the female; chicks take immediately to water. Both adults care for their young until they fledge 14 to 16 weeks later. Chicks will attain the characteristic bright white plumage within a year but will not nest until their fourth year. In fall, swans move south within family units and aggregate in areas where open water is available throughout the winter.

Expect to find these swans in lakes and beaver ponds during the summer and large rivers in winter. Trumpeter swans have been reintroduced in Minnesota, Wisconsin, and Michigan and are successfully breeding and expanding their range. Their estimated wild population is now over 6,000.

Common Merganser *(Mergus merganser)*
Hooded Merganser *(Lophodytes cucullatus)*
Common Goldeneye *(Bucephala clangula)*
Location: GL, NY, NE; Occupancy: S, M, W; Habitat Type: L, R; Population: S

Male common mergansers are striking birds that return early in spring to their former breeding territories. Hooded mergansers and common goldeneyes are also present as soon as the ice thaws from lakes and rivers. All three species can be found together and exhibit similar behaviors, particularly in their courtship rituals. These rituals serve to showcase multiple males to one or more females and are conducted en route to breeding territories. Once a pair arrives on a breeding lake

Common Merganser

Hooded Merganser

Common Goldeneye

or river, a nest site is located, generally in a large tree cavity. Mergansers may choose nest cavities up to one mile from the water. Such distances make for a dangerous escape route for young leaving the nest. Large tree cavities, however, are a rare commodity in recently cut forests, leaving fewer choices in the nest location.

Only the female incubates and raises the young. Males will stay in the general vicinity, but take no part in rearing the offspring. Outside of a few low grunts, adults are quite silent. Vocalizations are greatest when young

Common Loon

leave the nest. Low clucks by the female help orient young to the water, away from predators such as red fox, coyote, and fisher.

Expect to find mergansers and goldeneyes on open waters of lakes, rivers, and larger beaver ponds. All three species can be found on the Great Lakes.

Common Loon *(Gavia immer)* 🔊
Location: GL, NY, NE; Occupancy: S, M; Habitat Type: L; Population: S to D to I

Common loons have come to define much of the lure of the Northwoods region. Their calls have been described as haunting and beautiful, wild in nature, deep in lore. Native American traditions from this region are rich in loon mythology. Vocalizations are readily heard in the early spring and throughout the summer as loon pairs defend territories and young.

The language of loons is primarily comprised of four calls. The yodel call is a territorial song that is only given by the male. The wail is a contact call for loons to communicate with near or far neighbors. Wails are also used between mates to locate one another. The tremolo call, or "laugh" of the loon is an indicator of stress and anxiety. It is also the only call that is used in flight to determine occupancy by other loons on a lake below. The last call is a hoot. This is a familial, short-range contact call among family members. Loons will also use several variations of the above calls to communicate more complex expressions. These combinations are most dramatically heard during a night chorus. On large lakes or areas with clusters of many small lakes, multiple loon pairs will regularly communicate among one another. Night chorusing is a means to check on the status of other loons within the neighborhood. Loons prefer nesting along shorelines of islands or on bog mats. Nesting can begin in mid-May, but egg laying is more common in early June. Incubation requires both parents for a minimum of four weeks. Upon hatch, chicks almost immediately leave the nest. By seven to eight weeks, young are nearly independent and fledge at 11 to 12 weeks. In the fall, loons migrate independently of each other to ocean wintering areas.

Expect to find breeding loons on lakes over 60 acres with clear water, adequate supply of fish, and minimal shoreline development. Dedicated campaigns of loon awareness and protection have allowed successful breeding on more developed lakes.

American Bittern *(Botaurus lentiginosus)* 🔊
Location: GL, NY, NE; Occupancy: S, M;
Habitat Type: B, L; Population: S to D

More often heard than seen, the American bittern has a diagnostic deep gulping sound. This territorial call may be heard at any time of the day or night, primarily in large wetland habitats. Although the bittern is a fairly large bird, standing 28 inches high with over a three-foot wingspan, its streaked

American Bittern

coloration and cryptic behavior are effective in keeping it well camouflaged. When found, the bittern freezes and points its bill upward, attempting to mimic the surrounding vegetation. In this pose, the bittern can best utilize low-set eyes to watch an intruder. In late spring, loosely built stick nests are placed on the ground or perched above water. An average of four to five eggs are then incubated solely by the female for nearly one month. The chicks will remain here for their first two weeks. After this period, the female and her young move

Great Blue Heron

around the marsh feeding on aquatic prey, such as fish, frogs, crayfish, insects, and small mammals. Bitterns overwinter in the southeastern United States.

Expect to find this wading bird in wetlands. The bittern prefers a mix of open water that is edged with wetland vegetation.

Great Blue Heron (*Ardea herodias*) 🔊
Location: GL, NY, NE; Occupancy: S, M; Habitat Type: L, R; Population: S

The great blue heron is an imposing bird standing four feet high with a six foot wingspan. These wading birds are commonly found along the shorelines of lakes, ponds, and rivers. Much time is spent standing and staring, waiting for the right time to strike at prey such as fish, frogs, and small mammals. Great blue herons return to the Northwoods soon after ice-off. Heron pairs rarely nest on their own; instead, colonies of up to several hundred pairs are formed on islands or peninsulas surrounded by wetlands. Large stick nests are set high in deciduous and coniferous trees. Both the male and female incubate the three to five blue-green eggs for nearly one month. Young fledge in nine weeks but return to their nest to be fed for several more weeks. Herons migrate to the southern U.S. for winter.

Expect to find nesting colonies, or *rookeries*, throughout the Northwoods on islands and peninsulas. Disturbance of nesting colonies during incubation can cause abandonment. Forestry practices that provide 1,000 foot buffers with minimal disturbance during the nesting season are important for continued existence.

Osprey *(Pandion haliaeetus)* 🔊
Location: GL, NY, NE; Occupancy: S, M;
Habitat Type: L, R; Population: S

Ospreys are one of the most widespread birds in the world. They are strict fish-eaters, targeting shallow water species, including suckers, bowfin, and bass. Specially designed barbed footpads and long talons are configured to maximize fish capture and carrying abilities. Ospreys can plunge feet first into the water, grab a two- to four-pound fish, and regain flight composure without landing in the water. These raptors also have the ability to hover in one place, which aids in stabilizing them for flight after a plunge.

In late spring, large stick nests are placed at the top of both live and dead trees. Pairs

Osprey

will use telephone poles, old buildings, docks, and buoys. Following an osprey in flight is one way to locate a nest site, particularly if a fish is being carried. Incubation of three eggs is mostly by the female for a five- to six-week period, with the male delivering food to the nest. Chicks hatch nearly one week apart from each other in the order of their laying. Chick sizes can therefore vary greatly, and in years with low food availability, only one chick may survive. Ospreys start migrating in September and may fly as far south as Brazil for the winter.

Expect to find ospreys on lakes, including the Great Lakes, rivers, and the ocean. Ospreys give a series of high-pitched *kyew* calls while circling above a lake. A more pronounced version is used when alarmed or agitated. Osprey populations have rebounded from heavy exposure to DDT in the 1950s through the 1970s.

Bald Eagle *(Haliaetus leucocephalus)* 🔊
Location: GL, NY, NE; Occupancy: S, M, W; Habitat Type: L, R; Population: S to I

Bald Eagle

The bald eagle is a large, prominent fish-eating bird. An eagle's call is surprisingly guttural, often heard when nests are disturbed. Bald eagles are also opportunistic eaters. Some territorial pairs develop a taste for what is most common in their breeding territory, including Canada geese, squirrels, or horseshoe crabs. Eagles choose tall trees for nest sites, usually white pines that extend above the forest canopy. These sites are reused over decades and as such, nest bowls can amass to large sizes. In some case, nests can measure over 10 feet across and deep, and weigh several tons. Both adults feed and raise the one to three young. Eagle chicks require 12 weeks of care before fledging.

The bald eagle was severely impacted by pesticides causing their numbers to plummet in the 1960s and 1970s. Dedicated conservation efforts eventually brought this raptor back to sustainable levels, ultimately leading to their removal from the federally endangered and threatened species list in 2007. Eagles are now once again a common sight in many areas of the Northwoods.

Expect to find these birds breeding along lakes, including the Great Lakes, rivers, and the ocean. Winter roosts of many individuals are associated with open water. Look for the characteristic white head and tail of breeding adult eagles. Individuals less than four years of age are primarily brown.

Virginia Rail *(Rallus limicola)*
Sora *(Porzana carolina)*
Location: GL, NY, NE; Occupancy: S, M;
Habitat Type: L; Population: S to D

The Virginia rail and sora spend their days
concealed in emergent wetlands, shimmying
their narrow bodies between plant stems. As
such, these birds are more apt to be heard
than seen. Both species have characteristic
calls. The Virginia rail has several calls
including a repeated *kid-ick, kid-ick, kid-ick*
and a more common staccato-like grunting
call, given by pairs while dueting. The
sora's call is commonly associated with an
emphatic voicing of its name. These reclusive
birds become even harder to find once eggs
are laid. For both the Virginia rail and sora,
oven-like baskets of vegetation are constructed by both parents and will house
seven to 12 eggs for nearly three weeks. Both
adults will also share in the incubation duty.
Upon hatching, the fully feathered chicks
remain at the nest site for a few days. Chicks
are able to swim immediately after hatching
and are capable of flight in four weeks.

Both species migrate considerable
distances, well over 1,000 miles for some, to
their southern U.S. wintering areas. Migra-

Virginia Rail

Sora

65

tion occurs at night and at low altitudes, making these birds susceptible to collisions with cellular towers and even lighthouses.

Expect to find Virginia rails and soras well hidden among emergent vegetation in wetland areas. Often, a loud sound, such as hand clapping or a nearby train, can elicit rail calls from a marsh during May's peak vocal times.

Belted Kingfisher

Belted Kingfisher *(Megaceryle alcyon)* 🔊
Location: GL, NY, NE; Occupancy: S, M;
Habitat Type: L, R; Population: S

The belted kingfisher's loud rattling call can be heard across all waters of the Northwoods, whether at shallow beaver ponds, lakes, rivers, or even along the shorelines of the Great Lakes and Atlantic Ocean. The kingfisher's ability to adapt to such a diversity of habitat is only limited by suitable nest sites. Kingfishers nest in burrows dug from eroded ground. Riverbanks and lake shorelines are common areas for such nesting habitat. Other attractive sites include gravel pits, roadsides, dirt piles, and any other freshly excavated areas. By mid-April, males have returned from wintering areas and are soon followed by the females. Courtship is fleeting but includes the joint digging of a nest burrow. Such burrows are typically six feet long and have a three to four inch diameter. Both adults incubate the eggs and share in caring for the seven hatched young. Food deliveries by the adults average one every 15 to 30 minutes throughout the day. Fish, frogs, and crayfish are the favored diet. Six weeks after hatching, young make their first forays from the nest burrow. Kingfisher families remain together for two or more weeks after fledging. Males can stay on territory throughout the winter if feeding areas remain ice-free, but most kingfishers migrate south for the winter.

Expect to find kingfishers in nearly all open water habitats where the water is clear and small fish are common.

Painted Turtle

Snapping Turtle

North American Wood Turtle

Where are all of the Reptiles?

In the Northwoods, reptile species diversity is low. Only the hardiest species can survive winters in these woods. The garter snake is most commonly found, along with the redbelly and green snakes, both are small docile snakes rarely over a foot in length. Several turtles are also present. The three species of turtles

Green Snake

with the broadest ranges in this region are: the painted turtle, the snapping turtle (by far the largest species), and the relatively rare North American wood turtle. Wood turtles are a long-lived, terrestrial species best associated with sandy riverbanks where they lay an average of five to 13 eggs. An interest in making wood turtles pets has devastated their populations in the Northwoods and other regions.

Garter Snake

Fall

IN THE NORTHWOODS

It was Indian summer, a bluebird sort of day
as we call it in the North, warm and sunny,
without a breath of wind; the water was sky-blue,
the shores a bank of solid gold.

–Sigurd Olson

Swift Diamond River, New Hampshire

North American Porcupine *(Erethizon dorsatum)*
Location: GL, NY, NE; Occupancy: PR;
Habitat Type: P, SF, NH, WC; Population: S

The North American porcupine is a well known member of the Northwoods. This large rodent weighs up to 30 pounds and has little fear of predators. The porcupine's casual manner and lumbering movements reflect its natural armor—quills, up to 30,000 by some counts. These quills are modified hairs, up to two and one-half inches long, and are found on the backside of the porcupine. Since the face and belly

North American Porcupine

are unprotected, porcupines must tuck their head and back into an intruder when threatened. Porcupines are generalists in their habitat selection, ranging from coniferous to deciduous forests and even meadow edges. Leaves and buds of birch and aspen are favored summer foods, along with herbaceous growth including emergent wetland species. In winter, porcupines are less selective and focus on the inner bark of sugar maple, yellow birch, and hemlock. These animals are most active at night, and in winter use protected den sites, such as tree hollows or rock ledges.

Expect to find the porcupine most anywhere in the Northwoods, including camps and campgrounds where it searches for salty items to satisfy a craving for sodium.

American Beaver *(Castor canadensis)*
Location: GL, NY, NE; Occupancy: PR;
Habitat Type: B, NH, L, R; Population: S to I

The American beaver is the architect of the Northwoods relying on an ability to change its surroundings. Beavers require the safety of water for both their homes and to access food sources. Dams are constructed across narrow portions of streams using cut branches dragged into position along with mud and sod. Dam length varies greatly and can reach 300 feet or more in some locations. Backwater flooding from a dam enables beavers to build lodges free from the shoreline. Beaver lodges are also constructed from cut branches and mud. These structures can reach massive proportions of 16 feet high and 40 feet long, although most are half this size. Lodges, some up to four feet thick, provide protection for beaver families throughout the year. Another engineering feat of beavers is an ability to create travel channels. Channels up to a half-mile long, complete with small dams, are created to minimize risk while accessing remote food sources.

Beavers are strict vegetarians. They prefer the inner bark of aspen, but will eat other trees and aquatic vegetation. The characteristic beaver cutting of a tree showcases the action of their large incisors. In fall, beavers sink and secure caches of preferred food at the bottom of their home waters. Later in winter, these animals will venture from their lodges to access these stored foods.

Expect to find beavers across the Northwoods. Look for stick lodges surrounded by water or burrows dug and capped with

American Beaver

sticks along riverbanks. Listen for the familiar alarm slap of a beaver's flattened tail on the water surface.

Moose *(Alces americanus)*
Location: GL, NY, NE; Occupancy: PR;
Habitat Type: B, SF, NH, L, R, WC; Population: S to I

The moose is the largest inhabitant of the Northwoods. In these parts, males may stand up to six feet high at the shoulders and weigh up to 1,200 pounds. The four- to five-foot spread of a male's antlers makes it an imposing animal, especially during the fall breeding season. During the fall rut, bulls lose their velvet by rubbing trees with their antlers. At this time, these animals are more aggressive and seek to challenge other moose, animals and even people.

Moose are most commonly seen in lakes, ponds, and other wet areas feeding on aquatic plants such as sedges and pondweeds. Moose will even dive underwater to forage. The mosaic pattern of mixed young forest growth with aspen, fir, and spruce are also attractive habitats for moose. These areas are created

Moose

several years after logging activities. In winter, moose browse on saplings of aspen, birch, fir, mountain ash, willows, and dogwood.

Although moose populations were once locally extinct or reduced to small numbers at the turn of the twentieth century, reintroduction programs and natural reoccupation have now reestablished this large ungulate throughout much of its former Northwoods range.

Expect to find moose during the summer months near water and along roadsides where they meet their need for sodium from past winter salting of roads. Antlers are shed in winter and are an important source of calcium for many Northwoods mammals.

Sandhill Crane *(Grus canadensis)* 🔊
Location: GL; Occupancy: S, M;
Habitat Type: B, L, G; Population: I

Like many large birds, populations of sandhill cranes hit all-time lows in the early 1900s after decades of rapid habitat loss and indiscriminate shooting. This crane's cousin, the highly endangered whooping crane, almost completely disappeared. Well-publicized efforts saved the whooping crane, and similar conservation initiatives were also undertaken for the sandhill crane across the Great Lakes.

Today, this bird has reoccupied much of its former Northwoods breeding range.

The sandhill crane stands four feet high and has a wingspan of seven and one-half feet. In open areas of the Northwoods, their loud and resonant trumpeting call can carry for a mile or more. As the breeding season comes to an end, crane families of three to five individuals begin to gather in common locations, called *staging areas*. Moving south, cranes continue to gather with others creating larger and larger groups. In recent years, such migratory movements have fortunately become a more common sight. With the recent trend in warmer winters, many cranes may not migrate as far to their southern U.S. wintering grounds; currently over 10,000 cranes overwinter in eastern Tennessee.

Expect to find these cranes breeding primarily in the Great Lakes region, although exploratory pairs are colonizing more eastern areas in New York and even New England.

Sandhill Cranes

The Spectacle of Migration

There is symbolic as well as actual beauty in the migration of the birds...
There is something infinitely healing in the repeated refrains of nature,
the assurance that dawn comes after night, and spring after the winter...
—Rachel Carson

The phenomenon of animal migration is a response to changing seasons and food availability. Mammals and birds have the best known migrations. Thousands of caribou move across North America's tundra in search of food and suitable calving areas. Woodland caribou have shorter movements and do not form the massive herds of the Far North. The majority of birds from this region migrate south for the winter. Raptors, waterfowl, shorebirds, and many songbirds also make this journey. In winter, some species migrate to and overwinter in the Northwoods, including the rough-legged hawk, owls, northern shrike, finches, and snow bunting. Bats and butterflies also migrate; their movements are briefly discussed in the following pages.

Bats: Hidden Movements of the Night

In the Northwoods, another migration occurs in the fall under the dark of night. Several species of bats undertake specific migrations from their Northwoods homes to warmer wintering clines. The longest of these night migrations occur in three forest-dwelling species: the red bat, hoary bat, and silver-haired bat. These bats are rarely seen; instead of roosting in structures during the day, they roost in coniferous trees. They also differ in appearance than the "typical" brown bat, having longer fur and more coloration. Recently, efforts to document the potential impacts of wind turbines on migrating wildlife have found that the biggest impact may be on forest bats. Wind turbines in West Virginia and Pennsylvania have killed several thousand migrant hoary bats in a single fall. Because bats are long-lived, some as long as 30 years, this death toll is likely to have significant ramifications for bat populations.

Waterfowl: Sounds from Above 🔊

Large flocks of migrating waterfowl in the fall are a Northwoods tradition. The largest of these species, the Canada goose with a five-foot wingspan and the tundra swan with a seven-foot wingspan, are prominent overhead migrants. Of the numerous goose subspecies, only the giant Canada goose breeds in the Northwoods. In some areas, such as the eastern Upper Peninsula of Michigan, it is a common breeding species. This subspecies can form large flocks that gradually move south following areas of open water during the winter. Smaller and more northerly subspecies form large V-shaped formations as they travel overhead in October and November toward southern U.S. wintering areas.

Tundra swans also use characteristic V-shaped formations during long distance movements. Flocks of these birds move through the Northwoods in November,

Migrating Tundra Swans

heading toward Chesapeake Bay for the winter. Some breeding populations, such as those from Alaska's tundra, move over 4,000 miles to their wintering areas. The honking of Canada geese and the lesser known but equally diagnostic bugling of tundra swans are memorable Northwoods calls during the fall.

Diurnal Raptors: Soaring with Thermals

All Northwoods diurnal raptors migrate or disperse south from their breeding areas. The annual fall migration of eagles, falcons, hawks, osprey, and vultures is a significant natural phenomenon worth viewing. Many of these raptors follow the contours of mountain ridges and shorelines of the Great Lakes and Atlantic Ocean, as they require or prefer to soar on *thermals*—hot air generated from heated landscapes. Hundreds, and in some places, thousands of raptors such as the broad-winged hawk, make spiraling flights south as they work from the top of one thermal and soar to the bottom of the next. Raptors with shorter or broad wings, such as

Red-tailed Hawk

the sharp-shinned hawk and turkey vulture, have difficulty crossing large waterbodies or other areas that lack thermals. These species can be seen en mass at the corners of the Great Lakes, at certain mountain peaks, and along the Atlantic Coast. Species with longer and more pointed wings, such as the peregrine falcon and osprey, do not depend on thermals and therefore can be seen making open water crossings. The northern goshawk only moves as far south as needed to find sufficient prey throughout the winter, while ospreys may migrate as far south as the Amazon River basin.

Shorebirds: Testing Migration Limits

Shorebirds represent a diverse group with an assorted mix of migratory patterns. Some, like the least sandpiper, are small and move in large flocks of hundreds and even thousands. Others, like the much larger whimbrel, can be seen as lone individuals making their way south. While only a handful of shorebirds breed in the Northwoods, most shorebirds use the Northwoods for resting and feeding en route to their wintering grounds. The American golden plover, for example, flies a roundtrip migration route of over 20,000 miles, and uses the Northwoods as a staging area to prepare for the 2,500-mile flight over the Atlantic Ocean on its way to Argentina. All told, approximately 30 species may be found moving through the Northwoods during migration.

Butterflies: Monarch Travels

The monarch butterfly has a unique annual reproductive strategy that is dependent on four generations; three generations live six to eight weeks while the year's fourth generation lives four to five months. This longer-lived generation will undertake one long-distance migration, a winter hibernation, and a second and final short-distance migration.

Adult female monarchs in the Northwoods first lay 500 eggs in June on a key host plant: the common milkweed. Eggs hatch after four days into caterpillars that soon have a series of yellow, white, and black bands. These caterpillars solely eat milkweed leaves. In two weeks, they enter a *pupa* stage by forming a green chrysalis that hangs from under a milkweed leaf. The white sap in this plant is toxic to other animals, providing an additional protective measure. After 10 days in the chrysalis, the

The monarch caterpillar and adult butterfly

monarch metamorphoses into an adult butterfly. This cycle is repeated in July. Adults from this generation then make their remarkable migration, beginning in August. Individuals from the Northwoods can take over a month to migrate 2,000 miles to wintering areas in Mexico. Upon arrival, tens of millions of butterflies congregate in mature stands of oyamel firs. Many of these stands are now protected. In March, monarchs begin the long journey back to the Northwoods. These over-wintering adults, however, cannot migrate all the way back. Instead, they stop and breed in Texas and Oklahoma. Adults from this generation comprise the spring influx of monarch butterflies back to the Northwoods.

Winter

IN THE NORTHWOODS

A wind comes from the north
and blows out the sun.
Winter begins again.

–Gretel Ehrlich

Adirondack Park, Harrietstown, New York

Snowshoe Hare *(Lepus americanus)*
Location: GL, NY, NE; Occupancy: PR;
Habitat Type: SF, NH, WC; Population: S

The snowshoe hare has the unfortunate status of being an animal considered prey by every predator large enough to take it. Changes in this species' abundance can have a rippling effect on predator populations, such as lynx and coyote. In some parts of its range, hare numbers can vary from one to hundreds and even thousands of individuals per square mile. Every 10 years or so, peak densities of hare will occur, closely followed by peak predator densities. Snowshoe hare

Snowshoe Hare

prefer swamps with mixed coniferous and deciduous forests having a thick understory; such habitats include white cedar swamps, spruce-fir forests, and alder thickets. In winter, hares survive on the buds, twigs, and bark of birch, aspen, maple, cedar, and spruce.

Expect to find these hares browsing on the edges of small openings at crepuscular hours. In the summer, the snowshoe hare's white fur is replaced with a brown coat for more suitable camouflage. By winter, however, hares have changed back to white for optimizing their ability to blend with snow.

Canada Lynx *(Lynx canadensis)*
Location: GL, NY, NE; Occupancy: PR;
Habitat Type: SF, NH, WC; Population: D to S

Lynx are currently listed as a federally threatened species and are therefore rare in the U.S. Northwoods. Threats to these animals include trapping, habitat loss, and competition with bobcat. They are also vulnerable to incidental loss in traps. Lynx do not necessarily require wilderness areas; their presence is more strongly linked with habitats that support their primary prey, the snowshoe hare (see *Northwoods Spotlight – Predator-Prey relationships*). Mixed deciduous and coniferous forests with different aged stands of trees, including recent cut or burned areas are optimal for snowshoe hare, and therefore lynx. This habitat is also attractive to the far more adaptable and common bobcat. The large three and one-half-inch footprint and long legs of the lynx can provide a competitive edge over the bobcat in the Northwoods, as long as winters are cold with deep snow.

Expect to find the lynx tenuously surviving in parts of the Northwoods. Their presence in the Upper Great Lakes is inter-

Canada Lynx

Northwoods Spotlight

Predator-Prey Relationships

Although most predators are opportunistic in their prey selection, certain predator-prey relationships become so tightly connected that densities of prey species can actually control the survival and well being of the predator. In mammals, the Canada lynx/snowshoe hare is just such a relationship. Other documented predator-prey relationships connect fisher to North American porcupines and the American marten to red squirrels. Some predatory birds also have similar associations: the northern goshawk depends on ruffed grouse while the great gray owl is tied to vole populations.

Above: American Marten;
Right: Red Squirrel

mittent and related to incursions from Canadian lynx populations. The success of a 1989-1992 reintroduction effort in New York is still not quite known. In New England, Maine with a population of up to 500 individuals, is the best place to find lynx in the Northwoods.

Northern River Otter *(Lontra canadensis)*
Location: GL, NY, NE; Occupancy: PR;
Habitat Type: L, R; Population: I

The northern river otter is now a common resident of most aquatic ecosystems in the Northwoods, including coastal waters of

River Otter

the Great Lakes and the Atlantic Ocean. However, by the turn of the 20th century, otter and many other furbearers were overtrapped. As a result, otter populations completely disappeared in the southern fringes of the Northwoods. By the early to mid-1900s, state legislation provided the first protection for this furbearer. Reintroduction efforts further restored former abundance and distribution.

A prominent feature of the otter is energetic behavior, particularly apparent in winter. Otter travel over snow using loping gaits and will slide down hills on their bellies. Some ice glides can reach a distance of 25 feet or more. River otters have large home ranges, the extent of which is dictated by habitat quality, fellow otter densities, age, and time of year. Young males can wander over 100 miles. The river otter's diet is primarily dependent on fish, preferably slow-swimming species such as suckers. Otter also forage on clams, crayfish, and various frog and turtle species.

Expect to find river otter on Northwoods lakes searching for underwater prey. Otter commonly make sharp barking calls above the water while viewing their surroundings.

White-tailed Deer *(Odocoileus virginianus)*
Location: GL, NY, NE; Occupancy: PR;
Habitat Type: P, NH, WC, G; Population: S

The white-tailed deer is commonly found throughout the Northwoods region, though its historical presence is far from present-day abundance. The formerly extensive pine and spruce forests and deep snow favored moose and caribou. However, with the cutting of woods and active management of game species by wildlife agencies, artificially enhanced deer densities have led to the proliferation of this species in the Northwoods. Such intense management of deer herds has ramifications: high densities of deer in certain locales wipe out forest understory and have made some plants, such as the Canada yew, quite rare.

Winter is the most challenging season for the white-tailed deer. Most individuals collectively gather in favored areas, called "deer yards." Such preferred locations are typically in northern white cedar swamps, which provide both cover and food. Artificial feeding stations can help deer through winter months, although their value to sustainable deer herds varies according to management philosophies.

White-tailed Deer

Feeding wild birds is one of the most popular hobbies in the U.S. This hobby has increased awareness and appreciation for birds, and has influenced the geographic distribution of some species, such as the tufted titmouse and northern cardinal. Bird feeding also provides a way to monitor winter bird populations.

Common Redpoll

Cornell Lab of Ornithology's Project FeederWatch and the National Audubon Society's Christmas Bird Counts are two ways feeder birds are monitored. While some species, such as the black-backed woodpecker, gray jay, and boreal chickadee, are difficult to attract to traditional bird feeders, their southern counterparts, the hairy woodpecker, blue jay, and black-capped chickadee, are common visitors. Sunflower seeds will attract many of the finches, particularly the evening grosbeak and purple finch, while thistle seeds are preferred by flocks of American goldfinch, pine siskins, and common redpolls. Millet is a seed source preferred by sparrows, such as the dark-eyed junco and the winter-visiting American tree sparrow. Suet attracts woodpeckers and both the red-breasted and white-breasted nuthatches. Although the enhanced survival of birds through artificial feeding may seem unnatural, such feeding activities supplement natural food sources lost through development or other permanent changes in the landscape.

Expect to find white-tailed deer across much of the Northwoods, although it is more common and in sustainable populations in southern areas. In more northerly parts of the Northwoods, moose and in some areas caribou, outnumber deer.

Great Gray Owl *(Strix nebulosa)* 🔊

Location: GL; Occupancy: S, W;
Habitat Type: B, SF, NH, G; Population: S

The great gray owl is a bird of the deep boreal forests of Canada and Russia and therefore is not common in the Northwoods. However, whether breeding in northeastern Minnesota or wintering across the Northwoods' landscape, it is a bird deserving notice. Great gray owls are one of the largest owls in the world, standing 27 inches high with a wingspan of over four feet. This owl's large appearance is deceptive. The female weighs only three pounds, with much of her bulk being comprised of a thick coat of feathers. The great gray owl's prey selection also does not reflect its size. Small mammals, particularly voles, are the primary prey. This owl uses a "wait-and-see" method for hunting, perching itself on a tree at the edge of a meadow opening. Like many owls, the great gray uses exceptional eyesight as well as hearing to provide pinpoint accuracy. Using only sound, great gray owls can follow and pounce on a vole under the cover of snow. When capturing prey becomes difficult, from low densities or difficult snow conditions, this owl switches to day hunting.

Expect to find this nomadic owl throughout the Northwoods, although breeding only occurs in the Great Lakes region. In some years, large numbers of individuals make their way south in response to poor prey availability in more northern areas. Unlike many owls, the presence of a great gray owl is best determined by sight instead of sound. A series of deep and resonant *whoop* calls are occasionally heard.

Great Gray Owl

Northern Shrike (*Lanius excubitor*)
Location: GL, NY, NE; Occupancy: W;
Habitat Type: B, G; Population: S

The northern shrike is a predatory songbird. While other songbirds typically eat insects, seeds, and fruit, the shrike's prey emphasis is on small mammals and birds. This bird uses a distinctly hooked bill, similar to a raptor's bill, to tear pieces of prey. The shrike, however, lacks the talons of raptors that enable it to hold down prey. To compensate for this inadequacy, shrikes have the unusual habit of impaling prey on a sharp object like a thorn or barbed wire. This allows shrikes to prey on larger animals as well as "store" food for future use. Northern shrikes nest north of the Northwoods in the taiga of Canada and Alaska.

Expect to find this songbird only in the winter, often visiting bird feeders. Shrikes

Northern Shrike

Pine Grosbeak

prefer open habitats, perching on small trees and fence posts waiting for voles, mice, and small birds such as finches, sparrows and snow buntings.

Pine Grosbeak *(Pinicola enucleator)*
Location: GL, NY, NE; Occupancy: W;
Habitat Type: SF, NH; Population: S

The male pine grosbeak is a strikingly colorful finch, with a bright pink-red on its back and belly. Two white wingbars contrast with black wings. Females are gray with a yellow head. The pine grosbeak typifies the sporadic wandering abilities of northern finches. In some winters pine grosbeaks are sparse; however, when food supplies are limited in northern wintering habitats, this finch becomes more common across the Northwoods. Because individuals spend most of their lives in remote areas of the Canadian boreal forest and taiga zones, pine grosbeaks are quite tame and approachable.

Expect to find pine grosbeaks moving methodically while feeding on fruit shrubs, such as dogwoods, mountain ash, and crabapples. Pine grosbeaks are usually quiet and when they do call, they use soft whistled notes to communicate with one another.

Missing Members of the Northwoods

There is more to the holy north than loons.

–Jeff Fair

There are some species that have disappeared from the Northwoods—over hunted for their pelts or exterminated through ignorance. Although some furbearers like the fisher and marten were driven out of this region, they have benefited from reintroduction efforts. The rare and much larger wolverine has not been so fortunate and remains missing. The woodland caribou was once found in parts of the Northwoods at the end of the last century. While still found across the border in Canada, reintroduction efforts in Maine and Minnesota have not been successful. Mountain lion also once occupied these woods, yet today eastern populations are now considered extinct. Sightings of individuals and family groups, however, continue to spark hope of their possible existence in this region.

Golden Eagle

Birds, too, are also missing from these woods. Two former resident species include the whooping crane and golden eagle. Both were subjected to indiscriminant shooting, and in the case of the golden eagle, environmental contaminants appear to have played a significant role. Efforts are currently underway to return breeding whooping cranes to open bogs and wetlands of Wisconsin's Northwoods. Breeding golden eagle populations are now rebounding in eastern Quebec and could be a source for natural recolonization of old eyries in Maine.

The Northwoods landscape is incomplete without these and other missing species. Their return is not only important for functioning ecosystems but their presence restores a necessary wholeness. In this, the true spirit of the Northwoods is redeemed.

All good things are wild and free.

–Henry David Thoreau

Wolverine